C OAS
CIRCULAR
IN NORFOLK

Published & Distributed by Joy & Charles
Boldero, Thurning, Norfolk. July 1991.
Front Cover by Mike Bignold, Thurning.
    Photographs by Charles Boldero
Copyright Boldero Publishing. All rights
reserved.

British Library Cataloguing in Publication
Data.
Boldero Joy 1938 -
Coastal Circular Walks in Norfolk
1. Norfolk. Visitors' guides
1. Title 11. Boldero, Charles 1924-
        ISBN 0 9515478 3 6

Other Publications by the same author
include:-

CIRCULAR WALKS IN NORFOLK VOLUME ONE

MORE CIRCULAR WALKS IN NORFOLK

CHRONICLE OF A NORFOLK VILLAGE - THURNING

INDEX

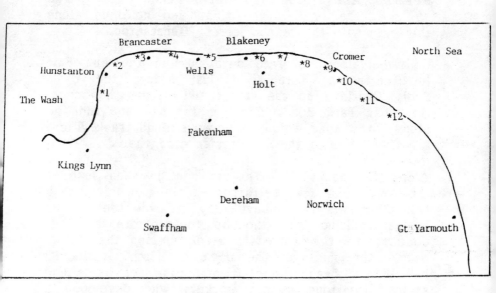

The maps in this book are diagrammatic and not strictly to scale.

------ Path   ːːːːː Track   ══════ Road

HEACHAM

(6½ MILES)

The paths on this walk are excellent and have the complete contrast of the windswept coastline of West Norfolk and quiet tracks through the countryside. Heacham is situated just off the A 149 two miles south of Hunstanton.

There is parking at the North Beach car park at Heacham.

START WALK From the North Beach car park go up onto the bank. Turn right and continue along this path with the sea on left to Hunstanton.

Continue along concrete path passing the Fun Fair in Hunstanton. Turn right just before the Oasis Pool. Continue up the street away from the beach. Go along Park Road. Cross main road and then go along Down Road which becomes a rough track. There are fine views of the countryside along here.

Along the banks wild flowers can be seen such as mallow with its heliotrope-pink flowers. Its a tall plant and in medieval days it was used as an anti-aphrodisiac and thought to promote a sober conduct! Its the white flowered campion that grows beside the mallow. The dock is often overlooked but it was used widely at one time for burns and scalds. Ironstone quarry workers who developed a peculiar type of sore on their arms would rub the fresh cut with a dock root. The Americans use it sprinkled with vinegar and then cooked it with ham.

At the junction of tracks turn right. As this track bears left keep straight ahead keeping cottages on left going uphill.

At the end of the wood, which is mainly beech, turn right along another track. Here there are extensive views of the coastline and ships can be seen on the horizon making for the port of King's Lynn. Dog roses grow in the hedgerow. Cross road and continue along track opposite. At the next road turn left with church on right and passing the Turret House.

The very restful church of St. Mary the Virgin is well worth visiting. One interesting memorial is over the south doorway and it is to those who drowned at Heacham in 1799. The party of twelve were visiting Capt. Pringle's ship the "Nile" lying off shore. There is also a memorial to Matoaka Rebecka Pocahontas, the daughter of Powhatan, the hereditary Overking of the Algonquin Indians of Virginia. She married in 1614 a John Rolfe who lived at Heacham Hall.

Turn right at road junction. Opposite is the Wheatsheaf Inn. The landlord welcomes walkers and has an extensive menu and several real ales. The Inn is open all day, but food is only served between 12 noon & 2p.m. and 6.30p.m. & 9p.m.

Keep along Station Road. At the fork take the North beach road back to start of the walk.

Heacham and Hunstanton are very popular seaside resorts. Heacham is now famous for its Lavender Farm which covers about 100 acres and stands on the A 149.

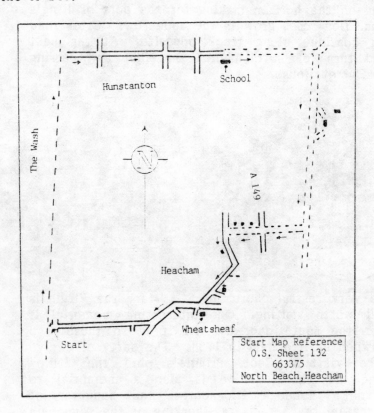

Start Map Reference
O.S. Sheet 132
663375
North Beach, Heacham

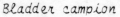

Bladder campion

Pineapple mayweed

HOLME NEXT THE SEA

(7 MILES)

This walk starts at Holme-next-the-Sea and goes inland over good tracks to Thornham and back via the Coastal Path to Holme.

There is parking available at Holme-next-the-Sea close to the beach. Holme is situated on the A 149 3 miles east of Hunstanton.

START WALK Walk along the exit path out of the car park and turn left along the country lane. Turn left taking the country lane through the attractive village with its pretty cottages.

The lovely church of St. Mary's is well worth a visit. One of the interesting items is the canopied alabaster monument to Richard Stone and his wife and family in the chancel. Members of the Nelson family are buried in the churchyard.

Cross the main road and continue along wide rough track opposite. In the banks many wild flowers can be found such as white and red dead nettle, alexanders, cow parsley and yarrow. The Anglo/Saxons thought that yarrow could heal wounds and it was known as woundwort.

Near the top of the hill there are extensive views of the countryside and coastline. Ringstead windmill is seen to the right. Turn left along the track. At the hedged country lane keep straight ahead, passing a trig point on left. At the T junction turn left.

Going down the hill into Thornham, Thornham Hall can be seen on the right. At T junction in the village turn right and at the Kings Head turn left into Church Street.

The King's Head welcomes walkers, serves a tasty bar meal and has a choice of several real ales. The opening hours are weekdays 11a.m. to 3p.m., 7p.m. to 11p.m. Sundays opening at 12 noon.

In this Saxon village of Thornham the houses are built of local chalk and brick. In the chalk pits many ice-age fossils have been found. The church has a beautiful screen. It was donated by a wealthy merchant, John Millar, in 1488. There are interesting carvings on the pew ends and a model of the 'post mill' that stood on high ground to the south of the village. When it was moved nearer the harbour the post was not re-erected. Instead the body was mounted on a short brick tower on which it could face the wind by the action of a fan carriage.

Thornham Hall

Continue along Church Street. Turn left along the Coastal Path with marker sign. Turn left over plank bridge going along a narrow path. In early summer the cuckoo can be heard. Reed birds inhabit the reed beds. Go over second bridge, cross road and up the bank. Turn right. The path continues alongside a staithe. Holme Church can be seen to the left.

In the creeks oyster catchers and redshank as well as many other waders can be seen feeding.

Continue along the coastal path. There are fine views of the beach and countryside. The Norfolk Ornithologist's lake and observation point are on the left.

From here you can either walk along the golden
sandy beach to just before the point, where we
suggest you rejoin the coastal path, or keep along
the coastal path going through the wooded area.
In the dunes sea lavender with bluish-purple
flowers can be found also samphire, a local
delicacy. The stalks are eaten like asparagus, the
leaves pickled in vinegar.

Keep to the right of the golf course and go along
a wide sandy track. At the Coastal Path sign turn
left along a wide wooden path back to the car
park.

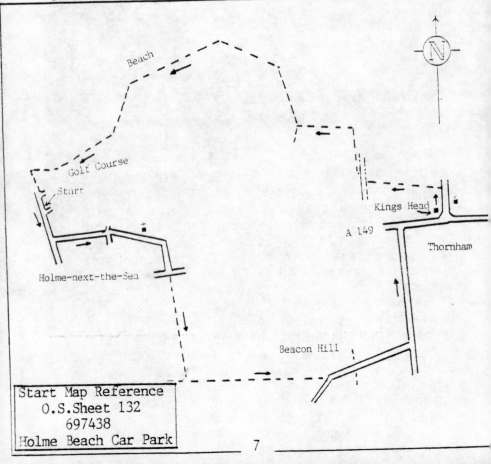

Beach

Golf Course

Start

Holme-next-the-Sea

Kings Head

A 149

Thornham

Beacon Hill

Start Map Reference
O.S.Sheet 132
697438
Holme Beach Car Park

7

BRANCASTER

(5½ MILES)

This walk has excellent paths and wild flowers abound in summer in the banks. Along the creeks waders and other birds can be seen. There is parking at the beach car park by the golf links at Brancaster which is situated on the A 149 five miles east of Hunstanton.

START WALK From the beach car park go away from the beach, cross road and take the path that goes behind the toilets. Continue along this path ignoring steps down to stile. The path goes over a mown area and behind houses then over a stile. Turn left at the track.

At the road turn right then left into Butchers Lane. On the left just after the corner and just before Sutherland Cottages turn left up a narrow path between walls.

At the lane turn right then left at metalled lane. Further along on the left is where the old Roman fort once stood. Its walls were 11ft thick backed by ramparts and a wide ditch. It was built to guard the approaches of the Wash. In the 3rd century it was a well fortified naval base with navy patrols. It was also a garrison for a calvary regiment.

THE NATIONAL TRUST

BRANODUNUM
ROMAN FORT

THE NATIONAL TRUST
OPEN TO THE PUBLIC
(SUBJECT TO THE BYELAWS
ON THE BACK OF THIS NOTICE)
PLEASE AVOID
LEAVING LITTER
LIGHTING FIRES
DAMAGING TREES
OR PLANTS

At the end of Stocking Lane cross main road and turn left along narrow path beside road. At the wide hedged track turn right. At the top there are fine views of the coastline.

In summer the red poppies abound also the white flowered bladder campion. Dog roses can be seen in the hedgerows and in the grass the red flowered clover and blue flowered germander speedwell. The name of the latter derives from the plants value in speeding the healing of wounds when applied to them.

At the top of the track is Barrow Common. Just after the notice turn sharp left along a narrow path that goes into a copse. Follow this path around until you reach the common again after passing old concrete structures on your left. Gorse and rosebay willowherb grow on the common as well as other wild flowers. Keep on the main path bearing left to the road. At the country lane turn left going down hill.

Germander speedwell

At the bottom of the hill stands The Jolly Sailors, a very friendly pub which welcomes walkers of all ages. We can recommend the fish pie. It also has many other tasty meals on offer.
In July and August it is open from 11a.m. to 10p.m. seven days a week for food. There are several real ales to choose from too.
Just down the road at Burnham Deepdale the landlord has self catering accommodation for walkers at Bunkhouse Barn. For more information Brancaster (0485) 210314.

Cross road and take footpath opposite. At the creeks turn left keeping the creeks on right. Bear left over roadway and just before the National Trust Information barn turn right along a very narrow path between wall and wire fence with Long Distance yellow marker.

Climb stile and continue along the coastal path. The boarded path ends and becomes an earth one. At road turn left and go through gateway. Turn right and follow this path back to start of the walk.

Walking beside the creeks there are many different kinds of birds to be spotted from waders to shell duck to reed birds. In the banks the rather rare plant, yellow rattle, grows. It name derives from the sound effect produced by the ripe seeds rattling in the pods. Its tube-like flowers are at the top of the hairy stem.

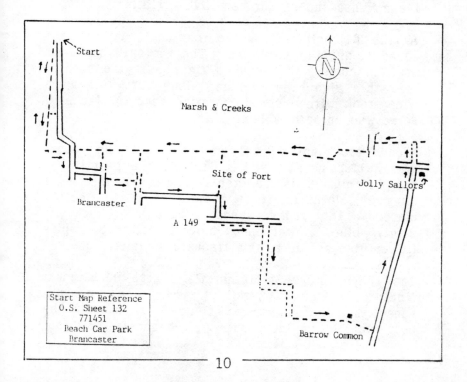

Start

Marsh & Creeks

N

Site of Fort

Jolly Sailors

Brancaster

A 149

Start Map Reference
O.S. Sheet 132
771451
Beach Car Park
Brancaster

Barrow Common

AROUND THE BURNHAMS

(4 or 6 MILES)

This route around the Burnhams would have been familiar to Lord Nelson whose home was at Burnham Thorpe. The paths on the whole are good and the walk takes you inland and also around the salt marshes where wading and other birds can be seen. There are many wild flowers in the banks and wet meadows.

START WALK: There is free parking at Burnham Norton which is situated just off the A 149 two miles north of Burnham Market.

From the car park go back to the road and turn left walking up through the pretty village with its flint cottages. There are fine views across the marshes and of Burnham Overy Mill.

At the T junction cross the road and keep straight ahead along track opposite. The footpath continues at field edge with hedge on right. At the country lane turn right then further along turn left up a wide track with a commemorative seat to Mackie & Peter who enjoyed walking here.

Along here many wild flowers grow including goose grass which geese love to eat. In the past it has been a missile in children's games as the seeds cling to clothing. It is a relative of the coffee plant. White campion and ground ivy with its dainty blue flower and clover with its white flower give colour to this track in summer.

The 13th century St Margaret's Church in Burnham Norton is well worth a visit. The colourful wineglass pulpit has been claimed as one of the best examples in the country. The panels show four doctors of the church, Ambrose, Augustine, Gregory and Jerome.

Just inside the door is the bread oven once used for baking wafers for Holy Communion, and on the other side a niche with a cinquefoil head, once used to hold a Holy Water stoup.

Turn right at the road and just after the Burnham Market village sign turn left along a narrow track between a wire fence and hedge. At the road turn right. On the opposite side of the road on the left are the remains of the Carmelite Friary. It was founded in 1241 by William de Calthorpe & Sir Roger de Hemenshale who both lived locally. The gateway is considered to be an important early example of Decorated flushwork.

At the T junction turn left passing the old mill. Continue right at the grass triangle with old stone cross.

Turn left into church yard.
Burnham Overy Town Norman
church has a wall painting
of St. Christopher carrying
the infant Jesus across the
water on the flight to Egypt
and many other interesting
gems.

Continue through the
churchyard and go through
the kissing gate into narrow
footpath with cottages on
left. At road turn right and
go along wide grass hedged
track. At T junction of tracks
turn left. Many wild flowers
are found here such as bladder
campion which flowers day and night but only at
night emits its pleasant clover-like scent.

The track leads to Burnham Overy Staithe and
becomes a metalled lane. Either side are cottages
with attractive gardens. At the end of Gong Lane
stands the friendly Hero pub. The landlord
welcomes walkers and has a good choice of menu.
Cross road going down East Harbour Way and follow
the road left alongside the staithe. It is a
favourite place for sailing craft. At the T
junction turn right, then along the field edge
with hedge on left beside the road.

At the footpath sign cross the field on the well
defined path and climb stile. Continues along the
path. The marshes and wet meadows have a multitude
of wild life with waders and other birds such as
swallows and owls.

Where the path goes right (this is where you can
extend the walk by two miles continue on this

13

path which curves around the marshes.

Otherwise go straight ahead down to the stile and take the path over the wet meadows back to the start of the walk.

The Burnham villages are an ancient settlement where medieval pottery has been found also a fine Saxon cruciform brooch from the Pagan period (c 600 A.D.) They spread along the valley of the River Burn.

A Dutchman was called in to start to drain the marshes but the work was completed by Thomas Telford, the famous canal builder, at the beginning of the 19th century.

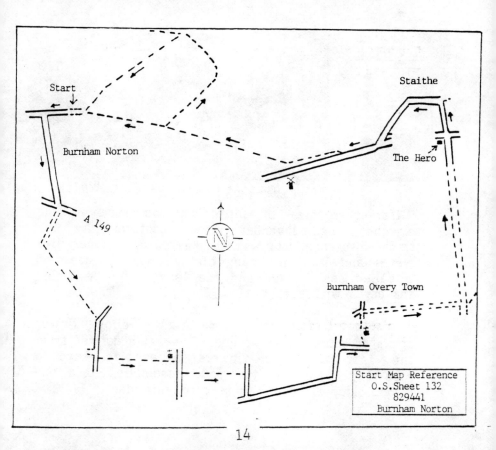

STIFFKEY

(5½ Miles)

There is free parking at the creeks. Drive along Greenway, a wide lane to the creeks. Stiffkey is situated on the A 149 mid way between Blakeney and Wells-next-the-Sea.

The paths on this walk are good with a mixture of coastline and countryside.

START WALK From the car park turn eastwards and keeping the creeks on the left go along wide footpath. Ignore wide track to right and continue along the main path which goes uphill.

Hide in memory of Bill Aldiss

Different species of birds can be seen in the marshes. Sea lavender grows profusely by the track also Sea beet which has wide leather like leaves and is a sprawling plant. In some areas it is called sea spinach and the leaves can be boiled and eaten with pork.

Bird's-foot-trefoil with its bright yellow flower grows on more mossy ground. The name derives from the fact that the flowers appear to have a shoe-shaped end of the pods resembling toes and claws. Skipper butterflies feed on this plant.

Further along the track on the horizon Blakeney Point can be seen and through binoculars seals on the sand banks.

The path goes up onto a high bank. Turn left here and after 10 yards turn right off the bank to stile. Cross meadow with river on left. Climb two more stiles and at road turn right.

Yellow, red, blue, and purple are the colours of the roadside banks in summer from the profusion of wild flowers. There are fine views of the coastline along here.

As the road bears right, cross it and go along narrow path opposite, between trees and river. Cross bridge and continue along the path under the avenue of willow trees. Cross bridge and go up Cockthorpe Common. At the top the path becomes a lane.

At the road turn right. (If you wish to visit the Toy Museum turn left for a few yards.) Continue along the road. At the brow of the hill there are fine views of the coastline. Go down hill and through Stiffkey with its pretty flinted cottages.

At the road junction turn left. At the old chapel turn right up track with footpath sign.

(150 yards further along the road is the Red Lion. We can recommend the food and beer there. The pub has an extensive blackboard menu.)

Where the track bends left go straight ahead through woodland and at the T junction of tracks turn left keeping the creeks on right back to start of walk.

Stiffkey is well known for its 'stewkey blues'

cockles! Because of the chemical re-action in the muddy sand the colours of the cockles range from dark blue to a pale blue.

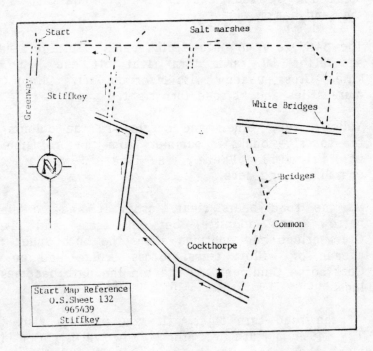

Common seal

SALTHOUSE

(3½ MILES)

This easy walk is all on well trodden footpaths and along the route wild flowers and many species of birds can be spotted.

Salthouse is situated on the A 149 five miles west of Sheringham.
There is free parking on the green.

START WALK Opposite the green by the red telephone box climb stile and go up hill along a narrow path. Climb stile and cross meadow, cross third stile and continue along well defined path in arable field.

Along here there are fine views of the coastline.

Climb stile, go down hill and climb another stile. Continue along well defined path through arable field. Go over bank then keep the hedgeline on left at edge of field.

At the corner of the field go slightly diagonally across field aiming for the clump of trees in the far right hand corner. (This public footpath is not so well used)

Turn right and go along narrow path between trees. You can take either of the paths to the right if you wish to visit the Norfolk Ornithologists Migration check point.

Cross road and turn left, then right along bank. Along here is a bird watcher's paradise. There are reed birds in the reeds, including the bittern, and waders on the ponds. If you wish to visit the hides tickets are available from the Norfolk

Naturalists shop further along the road on left.

At the end of the bank turn right. The North Sea is just the other side of the shingle bank.
Ignore the wide footpath to the right after passing two large ponds where avocets can be seen.

Along here thrift and sea bladder campion grow.

Just before the pill box bear right to stile.

Climb stile and go along wide grass path towards Salthouse. In the meadows hares can be spotted boxing.

Cross road and go up the lane. Go through the churchyard.

Turn right out of the churchyard along narrow path between trees. At the road turn right to start of walk.

The Dun Cow pub is very popular and welcomes walkers. They serve excellent hot and cold meals, with small portions for children. The real ales on sale include Websters.

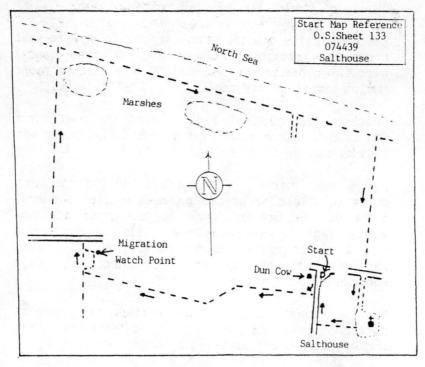

WEYBOURNE

(4 MILES)

This coastal walk starts at the car park by the beach at Weybourne which is situated just off the A 149 three miles west of Sheringham.

It has excellent paths with extensive views. Wild flowers and sea birds can be spotted on this walk.

START WALK From the car park turn left along shingle beach. This area is a favourite for fishermen, and dab amongst other fish are caught here.

To the left (the entrance is off the main road) is the Muckleburgh Museum which houses an extensive display of World War Two military hardware.

Keep along the coastal path. It was from here that the remote controlled 'Queen Bees' (target planes) were flown during the last war. Now a modern radar station stands on the spot.

Reaching the Quag at Kelling Hard the path turns left inland. Here heron, shell duck, moorhens and peewits can be found on the marshes.

Follow the winding path and turn left at junction of paths. Goldfinches can be seen in the hedgerow. Some of the flowers found in the banks are hog weed, ragwort and dandelions. This common weed, dandelion, is today grown commercially in France and sold in the markets. The dandelion plant contains a lot of vitamins A & C.

On the upper part of the nettles the peacock butterfly lays its eggs. The caterpillars when mature are velvety black with white spots.

At the road turn left, then right up a wide tree lined track passing a house on left. Continue uphill to the top, ignoring paths to the left. Honeysuckle grows in abundance here.

Cross wide track and continue straight ahead between gorse bushes. At the road turn left. Continue along the road down into Weybourne. Next to All Saints Church stand the ruins of the 12th century priory of the Augustinian Canons, of which only the tower remains intact.

The windmill is a land mark for miles around. There is a saying that runs "He who would old England win, must at Weybourne Hope begin".

Turn left at road junction passing the friendly
Ship Inn which has an extensive menu, real ale and
welcomes walkers. It is open (approximately) from
10.30p.m.-3.p.m. and 6.30p.m.-10p.m. for food.

Turn right into Beach Road and continue down the
road to start of walk.

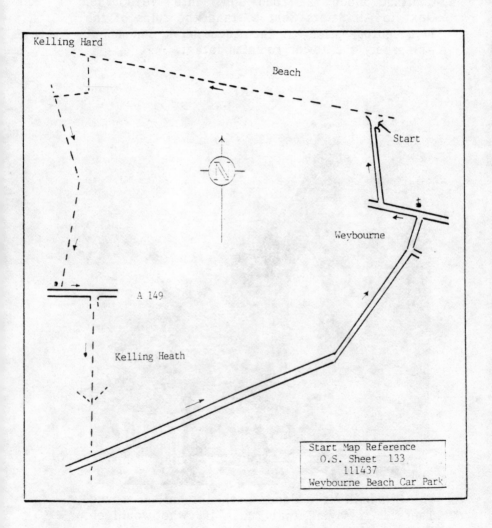

SHERINGHAM

(10 Miles)

This is the longest of the coastal walks and it has excellent paths. There is a large car park at the station (North Norfolk Railway) in Sheringham. Sheringham is situated on the A 149 4 miles west of Cromer.

START WALK From the car park walk through the town to the sea front. Turn left and walk along the promenade. Go up the steep path and at the top turn right then left keeping the coast on right.

The path narrows and goes alongside the golf course on left. There are extensive views of the coast and countryside along here.

Thrift and wild mignonette with its yellow flower grow in profusion along this path.

At the track turn left passing the windmill. At the road turn right.

(75 yards from the church corner is the Ship Inn. This friendly pub welcomes walkers and is open from 10.30am to 3.00p.m. 6.30p.m. to 10.00p.m. (approximately) seven days a week. It has an extensive menu and real ales.)

Turn left opposite the church then left again. Go
up Sandy Hill Lane passing the Weybourne railway
station on left.

Turn left at the entrance to Weybourne Forest
Lodge and then immediately right at the forestry
footpath sign and follow the footpath signs
through the wood.

Climb stile and at the caravan park turn right.
Continue along the main path through the caravan
park. This path veers right and then continues
along a very wide track to road.

At the main road turn right then left into
Allotments Lane, a track between field and tree
hedge then between dwellings.

At the road in West Beckham turn right and at T
junction turn left passing the Wheatsheaf pub on
left.

Take the left fork with church on right and
continue along the country lane. At the T junction
of roads go straight ahead up track.

At the road turn left and then right up 'by road'.
Turn left up track.

Honeysuckle grows in the hedgerows here as well as
many wild flowers in the banks.

Cross main road and go along narrow footpath
opposite. Ignore all footpaths to right and left
and keep along the main path. Foxgloves in their
many colours grow in profusion here.

The path veers right and then goes down hill
passing bungalow on left. Cross track and go along
track. There is a good view of the coastline along
here.

As the row of cottages face you turn left then
cross main road and take the path opposite with
yellow arrow sign.

Keep along this path which soon runs parallel to
the railway line on your right. Turn left into the
road then right. Keep straight ahead down path
which narrows with stream on left.

Cross common, turn right and go under railway
bridge. Take the left hand path over common with
houses to the left.

Path narrows between houses with stream first on
left then on right. At the road turn left and left
again and then right into Barford Road.

After sharp bends right, left and further along
right again, turn left then left again and walk
back to start of walk.

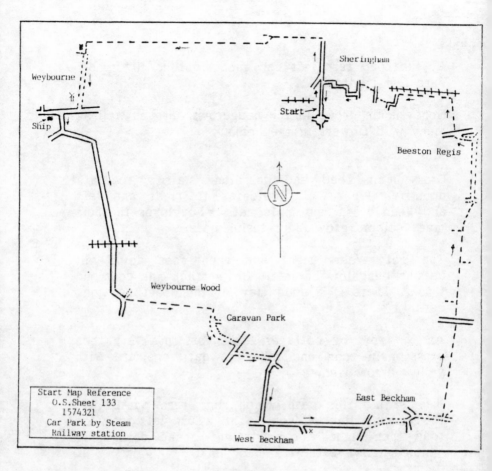

Weybourne

Ship

Sheringham

Start→

Beeston Regis

Weybourne Wood

Caravan Park

East Beckham

West Beckham

Start Map Reference
O.S.Sheet 133
1574321
Car Park by Steam
Railway station

Honey suckle

Red campion

Dog rose

CROMER

(4½ miles)

Cromer is well known for its crabs. The history of crab fishing as well as many other interesting facets of Cromer life can be found in the local museum. Cromer was first famous as a watering place in the 19th century. At that time there were bathing machines on the beach and very strict rules for bathing!

START WALK This coastal walk starts at the pier and you can take the path along the beach to Runton, or go on a higher path. (Except on the very highest of tides you can walk along the beach but it is advisable to check it out first)

With the pier behind you walk in a westerly direction. Go along path and just after the children's amusement area turn sharp left up hill. (If taking the beach path keep straight ahead) At the Melbourne Hotel turn right along the promenade. Further along the sunken gardens and putting green are on the left.

Cromer was mentioned in Jane Austen's novel 'Emma'. There used to be a prosperous town called Shipden situated on the seaward side of Crowsmere

as Cromer used to be called. It disappeared into
the sea in the 14th century. At very low tides a
large rock can seen several hundred yards out to
sea from the pier. This is locally known as Church
Rock, where the remains of the church of St. Peter
stood. The local story says that bells can be
heard to chime in stormy weather!

The wild plant Alexander only grows near the
coast. This herb with its greenish-yellow flower
is edible. The dark green leaves were used in
white sauces; the young stems can be eaten like
asparagus, the flower buds used in salads and the
roots used as a substitute for parsnip.

Continue along the grass footpath. There are fine
views of the coastline and inland views of Roman
Camp. Turn right down steps onto beach and then
left along beach. Where a concrete steepish path
comes into view on left keep along concrete path
straight ahead and turn left at toilets going up a
narrow path with steps.

Continue up the road and turn right at T junction
going through East Runton. Along here are two
inns, the White Horse and the Fishing Boat, both
of which serve food.

Cross road and keep along pavement. Opposite the
Gold Coast Caravan Park go along narrow tree lined
path on left. The path goes uphill passing Forge
Cottage with its anvil, hammer and tongs set in
the wall. Along here honeysuckle and lords &
ladies grow. In Elizabethan times the roots of
lords & ladies were gathered for their high starch
content, and were used for stiffening the high
pleated line ruffs.

The path goes over the railway line by way of the
stone bridge. At T junction of paths turn right
going slightly uphill. At the top of the incline

by the green notice turn sharp left along a sandy path. Gorse bushes cover a lot of Incleborough Hill which stands to the right behind you as you turn left. In spring it is a sight to behold. The farmer allows walkers to cross the field to the stile and climb Incleborough Hill (see the green notice) and from the top magnificent views can be seen.

Continue along the sandy track. The path goes downhill between trees. At the bottom turn right with the large green of West Runton on left.
Continue along the country lane. Take the left fork going along the narrow hedged path. In the hedgerow wild flowers abound. Cross road and go under railway bridge and up the track which becomes a metalled one.

Turn left and go over railway line via stone bridge turning right at T junction of paths. At the footpath sign turn left going over Howard's Hill which in spring is covered with the yellow flowers of the gorse.

At the end of the path on the right is where Cromer's zoo once stood. Turn right at road and between numbers 78 and 76 turn left along narrow alleyway.

At the road turn right and then left along Macdonalds Road. Cross main road and go up steps. Turn right through the gardens. Retrace steps back to the pier.

The cliffs at Cromer are eroding away but they are very well known from a geological view point, and have some of the finest illustrations of glacial deposits in the world. More information can be found in the museum which opens Monday to Saturday 10a.m. to 5p.m. (closing lunchtime on Mondays) and on Sunday 2p.m. to 5p.m.

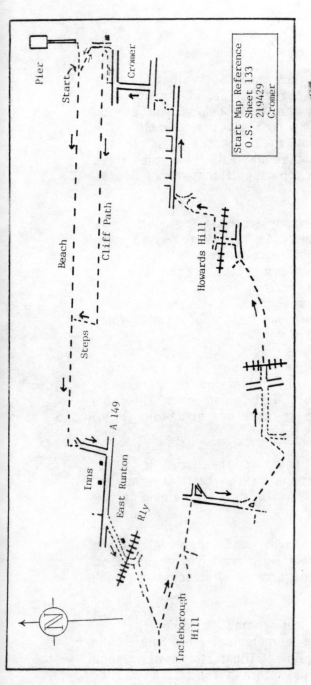

Start Map Reference
O.S. Sheet 133
219429
Cromer

31

OVERSTRAND

(7 Miles)

Part of this coastal walk is along the beach, and is walkable except at very high tides. There is car parking available at the seaward end of Paul's Lane, Overstrand which is situated on the B 1159 three miles east of Cromer.

START WALK Turn left out of the car park and then left again down concrete path to beach. Go along beach nearly to Cromer. Turn up left onto steep path with steps which winds around until it reaches the top of the cliff.

At the top turn left and just after play area turn right down a narrow path with trees. The path then climbs a little. Ignore path to right.

Cross road and go along Cliff Road and by the Spa shop turn left, then go right with a play area on left. Continue along Station Road going over railway bridges. Just after the garage on right turn left into country lane. At T junction turn right.(opposite road to Overstrand Hall). Go under railway bridge and at T junction turn left.

Turn right into narrow metalled lane then along narrow footpath with sign. Go left at T junction with tracks. The track widens and you go over another railway bridge. Along here there are many wild flowers and quite often a 'robins pin cushion' can be seen on the downy rose. The gall wasp punctures the plant and deposits its eggs producing a tufted growth which is bright orange/red.

Passing Northrepps airstrip on left and just before house turn left at footpath sign going up a narrow path. Turn right at sign and follow the

path to the church. Fat hen grows here; not the
farmers favourite but good to eat as it contains
vitamin B1 & 2 and calcium. It grows to about 3ft
high and can have reddish streaked stems, and the
flower spike is leafy.

Go over stile, through churchyard and at the road
turn left. The lovely church which is said to have
stood on this spot for 900 years has a beautiful
rood screen amongst its many gems.

Walk through this very attractive village where at
the local foundry the Gallas plough was invented
in the 19th century. At the T junction where a
fine thatched cottage stands turn left.

(50 yards up the road to the right is the Foundry
Inn. This friendly inn welcomes walkers and has a
good menu and real ale.)

At the village sign bear right along Bull Row then
as the track bends right turn left into track

keeping cottage on right. Continue up the track.
Turn right along a very narrow path with sign
between trees. The path descends and at T junction
of tracks keep left and keep along it to end.

Cross road and go along narrow path opposite. Turn
right into Paul's Lane and continue along it back
to start of walk.

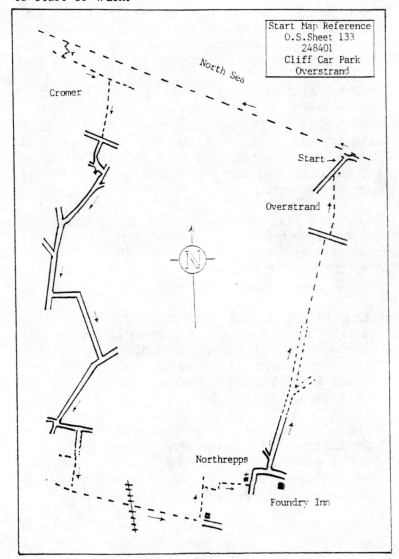

TRIMINGHAM

(7 MILES)

This is a pleasant walk, half of it along the beach and the other half inland over fields and tracks.

There is free parking in the wide lay-by on the west side of Trimingham just past the 30 mile an hour signs. Trimingham is situated on the B 1159 three miles east of Cromer.

START WALK From the lay-by go left along track between hedge and field. The path continues across the field and through a copse. In the copse campion and dock grow as well as other wild flowers. Dock leaves were once used to heal burns and scalds; today they are useful to rub away the sting of the nettle.

The narrow path descends steeply to the beach and can be slippery if wet. Reaching the beach turn right heading for Mundesley. The higher tides can cover parts of the beach at times. There is room to walk behind the sea defences.

Ignore the first slip road on the right to the beach. This beach is a favourite place for fishermen. Leave the beach by going up steep wide concrete path with iron railings. At the top turn left and keep the Trafalgar Court on right. At the road in Mundesley turn left.

It is said that the 'Long Coastguardsman' walks from Bacton to Mundesley every night just as the clock is striking midnight, but cannot be seen on moonlit nights. He loves wind and storms and is then heard singing or laughing.

Opposite the church turn right down Church Lane then right into Links road. Continue along the

Links Road. The hospital, built in 1899 was a
sanatorium for tuberculosis sufferers; now its a
convalescent hospital. At the footpath sign, soon
after a seat and sharp bend, turn right and go
through hedge gap. Follow path at edge of field by
the golf course.

At the end of the hedgeline go straight across
field. Continue along footpath at edge of field
going through a meadow and another field until you
reach the village of Gimingham. There are fine
views of the coastline along here.

GIMINGHAM

At this historic village street turn left, walking
at first alongside the river Mun where geese, duck
and moorhens can be seen. The mill was burnt down
in 1979 and rebuilt as a house. The area beyond
the river is said to be part of a 'stew pond', a
breeding place for fish for the monastery in days
past.

The church is well worth a visit with its 15th
century holy water stoup in the porch. There are
lovely stained glass windows in the chancel. The
font also dates from the 15th century.

Continue along the road. Turn right by the village
sign into Hall Road. Just outside the village turn
right along track opposite large barn and go
through farmyard. The path veers to the left. Go
through second gateway on right and across meadow
aiming for the bottom left hand corner. Go over
earth bridge and bear to the right of the field.
Go over rickety plank bridge over ditch. Climb
rickety stile and bridge over a wider ditch.

Turn right then after a short distance, left over
earth bridge. Turn left keeping ditch on left. The
footpath continues right, up the field, and
alongside hedge line on left. At lane turn right.
Opposite flint barn turn left going uphill along
the track by footpath sign. There are fine views
of the countryside from the top of the track.

Cross lane and continue straight ahead going over old railway bridge. At road turn right and at the main road turn left walking through Trimingham past the village sign to the start of the walk.

The church is worth a moment of time. Amongst its gems is the fine painted screen. It was lost, but found in a farm barn and restored in 1855.

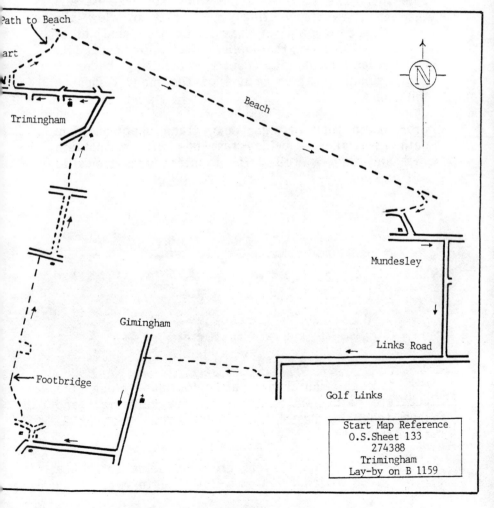

BACTON

(4 MILES)

This walk has good paths and there is limited parking on the Beach Road in Bacton Green which is situated of the B 1159 three miles southeast of Mundesley.

START WALK Go away from the beach towards The Ship Inn. The landlord there welcomes walkers and the inn is worth visiting for a pint to view the magnificent display of naval pictures and other naval artifacts on the walls. Keith Floyd of T.V. fame recommends the chef's speciality, bacon & onion dumpling which is one of the many dishes on the menu.

Cross main road and go along track opposite. The path at first is a wide grass one with a footpath sign and then a well defined path across fields to the church.

Go through churchyard and continue along the concrete path. At the country lane turn right and then take the Paston road passing the Bacton Gas terminal.

In the banks wild flowers grow including sorrel, a tall plant with reddish flowers. It was once prized as a vegetable. It is very good for removing ink stains, this is due to the oxalic acid in the plant. Amongst the sorrel are mallow, buttercups and sow thistle, another tall plant with yellow flowers. The leaves have a jagged edge. The hollow stems used to be given to sows to increase their milk yield.

At the main road turn left.

On the left is the famous 16th century Paston Barn. The church has 14th century wall paintings and fine stained glass windows and many other fine gems. The Paston family came to live in Paston in the 11th century. The family started the Paston School in North Walsham, but the name is famous for the 'Patson letters'. These were written by members of the family during the reign of Henry VI and Edward IV and they are an important and historic insight into life in those days.

Turn right into 'Loop Road' and at the track with footpath sign turn right again. Go along the well defined path in arable field. Then keeping the bank on right continue at field edge. At footpath sign go over bank and then along footpath at field edge. Turn left along wide grass track then over a wide gap in bank turn right and keep along this coastal path with sea and sandy beach below on left to its end.

Wild flowers abound here. Vipers-bugloss, a tall plant with beautiful blue flowers down its stem; Weld also tall with a yellowy-green flower. It was used in the middle ages by dyers as a yellow dye. Pineapple weed hugs the ground and the domed greenish-yellow flower looks a bit like a pineapple; it also gives off a scent very similar to a pineapple.

Bear left down path to the beach and keeping the sea on left walk along this sandy beach. By a lifebuoy take the path that goes off the beach and keeping the beach still on your left continue along the higher path with caravans on right. Ignore the first turning right and take the second one with a 'toilet' sign back to start of the walk.

There is supposed to be a ghost at Bacton named Jacob. He is dressed in a black monk's habit. The priory was founded in AD 1113 and was mentioned by Chaucer in his Canterbury Tales.

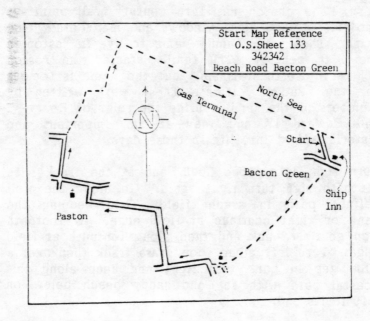